The Arab Americans

BOB TEMPLE

WE CAME TO AMERICA

MASON CREST PUBLISHERS • PHILADELPHIA

An Arab man rides a camel as the sun sets over a mosque. Most Arabs live in the large region between Europe, Africa, and Asia called the Middle East. Like other immigrant groups, they came to America searching for opportunities they could not find in their homelands.

The Arab Americans

BOB TEMPLE

WE CAME TO AMERICA

MASON CREST PUBLISHERS • PHILADELPHIA

Mason Crest Publishers
370 Reed Road
Broomall PA 19008
www.masoncrest.com

Copyright © 2003 by Mason Crest Publishers. All rights reserved.

First printing

1 3 5 7 9 8 6 4 2

Library of Congress Cataloging-in-Publication Data
on file at the Library of Congress

ISBN 1-59084-102-6

Table of Contents

WE CAME TO AMERICA

America's Ethnic Heritage

Barry Moreno, librarian

Statue of Liberty/

Ellis Island National Monument

Ethnic diversity is one of the most striking characteristics of the American identity. In the United States the Bureau of the Census officially recognizes 122 different ethnic groups. North America's population had grown by leaps and bounds, starting with the American Indian tribes and nations—the continent's original people—and increasing with the arrival of the European colonial migrants who came to these shores during the 16th and 17th centuries. Since then, millions of immigrants have come to America from every corner of the world.

But the passage of generations and the great distance of America from the "Old World"—Europe, Africa, and Asia—has in some cases separated immigrant peoples from their roots. The struggle to succeed in America made it easy to forget past traditions. Further, the American spirit of freedom, individualism, and equality gave Americans a perspective quite different from the view of life shared by residents of the Old World.

Immigrants of the 19th and 20th centuries recognized this at once. Many tried to "Americanize" themselves by tossing away their peasant clothes and dressing American-style even before reaching their new homes in the cities or the countryside of America. It was not so easy to become part of America's culture, however. For many immigrants, learning English was quite a hurdle. In fact, most older immigrants clung to the old ways, preferring to speak their native languages and follow their familiar customs and traditions. This was easy to do when ethnic neighborhoods abounded in large North American cities like New York, Montreal, Philadelphia, Chicago, Toronto, Boston, Cleveland, St. Louis, New Orleans and San Francisco. In rural areas, farm families—many of them Scandinavian, German, or Czech—established their own tightly knit communities. Thus foreign languages and dialects, religious beliefs, Old World customs, and certain class distinctions flourished.

The most striking changes occurred among the children of immigrants, whose hopes and dreams were different from those of their parents. They began breaking away from the Old World customs, perhaps as a reaction to the embarrassment of being labeled "foreigner." They badly wanted to be Americans, and assimilated more easily than their parents and grandparents. They learned to speak English without a foreign accent, to dress and act like other Americans. The assimilation of the children of immigrants was encouraged by social contact—games, schools, jobs, and military service—which further broke down the barriers between immigrant groups and hastened the process of Americanization. Along the way, many family traditions were lost or abandoned.

Today, the pride that Americans have in their ethnic roots is one of the abiding strengths of both the United States and Canada. It shows that the theory which called America a "melting pot" of the world's people was never really true. The thought that a single "American" would emerge from the combination of these peoples has never happened, for Americans have grown more reluctant than ever before to forget the struggles of their ethnic forefathers. The growth of cultural studies and genealogical research indicates that Americans are anxious not to entirely lose this identity, whether it is English, French, Chinese, African, Mexican, or some other group. There is an interest in tracing back the family line as far as records or memory will take them. In a sense, this has made Americans a divided people; proud to be Americans, but proud also of their ethnic roots.

As a result, many Americans have welcomed a new identity, that of the hyphenated American. This unique description has grown in usage over the years and continues to grow as more Americans recognize the importance of family heritage. In the end, this is an appreciation of America's great cultural heritage and its richness of its variety.

A group of Muslim men pray in a mosque in Baghdad, Iraq. During the early 20th century, many Arabs were forced to leave their homelands in order to make money to support their families.

1 An Immigrant's Story

As the 1900s dawned in the Middle East, the people in the countries that are considered Arab lands were looking to North America—specifically the United States—for new opportunity. They faced many struggles in their own land, among them suffering at the hands of the *Turks* who were in power at the time. Some faced religious *persecution* or *discrimination*. Others fought huge economic burdens, including heavy taxation. Some simply had heard about a better life and wanted the chance to pursue it.

One man left his homeland in pursuit of a better life and more freedom. He found his way from Lebanon all the way to Detroit, Michigan. His story was told by Abdo Elkholy in *Arab Moslems in the United States*:

> His reasons for leaving his country, Lebanon, or Syria as it was then called, were political and economic. Syria at that time was, among many Middle Eastern countries, a part of the Ottoman Empire whose satellites suffered and bore heavy burdens of political submission, social inferiority to the Turkish ruling class, and economic obligations. Everything was heavily taxed, even one's own garment; not more than one member at a time of the large family could go outside or walk in the street, for the garment had to be sealed to indicate the tax payment.

This man, like many other *immigrants* of the time, also had religious concerns. As a *Muslim*, he was probably finding himself at odds with the largely Christian European governments of France and Britain that had gained a stronghold in the region at the time. Muslims were the majority in Arab lands, and the Ottoman rulers were Muslim as well. But economic concerns led to his departure.

> The main reason for the emigration…was the economic misery prevailing in his country. He was 25 years old and mature enough to think of escaping his unhappy fate. He saved a few liras, which enabled him to buy his ticket to join some friends on a boat to America in 1902. He did not know where he was going.

He ended up being quite lucky. Unlike many of his peers, who were *duped* into boarding boats they believed to be headed for America only to wind up on a completely different continent, this man landed in New York City. His journey was most likely rough and extremely unpleasant. He was probably loaded into *steerage* like so many cattle, crammed in with other Arabs with big dreams. During the weeks-long journey, he probably endured hardships ranging from lack of food to unsanitary conditions. Depending on the length of his journey and the number of people on board, he likely witnessed a few passenger deaths. He undoubtedly kept his spirits up with dreams of the possibilities that awaited him—dreams based on stories he had heard from relatives who had gone ahead of him.

The Dome of the Rock in Jerusalem is one of Islam's holy centers. People of the Islamic, Jewish, and Christian faiths consider Jerusalem a sacred city. The wall in the foreground is part of the ancient Jewish temple.

A Palestinian boy holds up a toy pistol and a rock. Conflict between Palestinians and Jews has existed since before the 1948 foundation of Israel in the land called Palestine.

Knowing no English, he *affiliated* himself with some Syrian Christians walking from New York City and followed their occupational pattern of *peddling*, walking from one state to another. By the end of the year he found himself in another Syrian Christian community in Detroit. He settled down there as one of the city's few Moslems. In 1905, he heard of some relatives who had come from Syria and immediately paid them a visit, returning with a 15-year-old wife, who, during their marriage bore him six children—three boys and three girls.

His plan was simple: Come to America, *capitalize* on the prosperity that could be found in abundance here, then return to his homeland and live a life of leisure. Most of his fellow Arabs found life much to their liking in the United States and, instead of returning home, sent money home to allow their relatives to follow them to the New World. This man, however, never gave up the dream of returning home. His children, on the other hand, became Americanized, losing much of their heritage in the process.

Like many Detroit-area Arabs of the time, he worked in a factory, performing unskilled labor. He never did earn enough money to return to the homeland, and his children quickly grew, marrying outside of the Arab culture and, in some cases, becoming Christians. It was common in this era for second-generation Arabs (and other *ethnic* groups) to become blended into the fabric of American society.

Later in their lives, his children and grandchildren returned to their roots and sought to rediscover traditional Arab culture to some degree.

This man had been part of the first of two big waves of immigration from Arab lands to North America. With the second wave, which occurred after World War II, Arab culture became revived in America because American culture was more open to accept it. ✴

An Arab infant wears ornamental hairpieces in this photograph, taken near Nasiriya, Iraq.

An Arab Boy Scout uses a blade of grass to tickle his friend's ear. The Boy Scouts are an international organization, so there are scout troops in the Arab countries just as there are troops in the United States and Canada.

The First Wave

From the 15th century until the end of World War I, the part of the Middle East that includes Syria, Lebanon, Palestine, Jordan, Iraq, and part of northern Africa was ruled by Turkey, which was then called the Ottoman Empire. In general, people from any of these areas during this time were known as Turks, or sometimes as Syrians. However, many people who have been classified as Syrians were actually from Lebanon, Palestine, or other countries in the region.

Immigration to the United States from these Arab lands came in two distinct waves. The first group of immigrants came at the end of the 1800s through the beginning of World War I; the second group came after World War II, especially after 1967.

A number of factors were key in the first wave of immigration to North America, but the biggest reason appears to have been religious, although economic factors undoubtedly played a role as well. The majority of immigrants during this period, which ran roughly from 1885 to 1914, were poor, uneducated, and lived in rural areas. They were caught in an era of Ottoman rule and religious *strife* that led to many bloody battles.

The religious strife was not simply a battle between Christians and Muslims, although that contributed greatly to the situation. In fact, both religions had become fractured into several major divisions.

Christians of this time were either Maronites or Melkites, both of which were Roman Catholic. Another faction, the Syrian Orthodox Christians, was part of the Byzantine church. Muslims were divided into three groups: Sunni, Shiah, and Druze.

The Ottoman rulers were Muslims themselves, which caused the Christians of the time to suffer through persecution and discrimination.

Because most Arabs follow Islam, some people believe all Arabs are Muslims. However, there are many Christian Arabs as well. These Christian Arabs are carrying a cross through the streets of Jerusalem as part of a Good Friday celebration.

Christian Arabs were also being influenced by Americans through the American Christian Ministries, which opened schools and churches to serve the population in this area. They also provided food and built hospitals. It is believed that the commitment these American Christians showed to the area had a lasting impression on some of the Syrian Christians they served. In fact, it may have overinflated the impression of the Arab people about life in the United States, giving them the feeling that all Americans were as committed and caring as the volunteers were. Also during this period, the Ottoman Empire began to crumble, and Britain and France gained influence in the region. These Europeans also favored the Christians, who were a minority in the area at the time. This drove a wedge between the Christians and Muslims, who had managed to co-exist for centuries, and caused more hostility between them.

But it wasn't only religious strife that brought this first wave of Arab immigrants in such huge numbers. Economic factors played a role, although a much different role than for similar immigrants from other countries. Many ethnic groups of this era headed to America as a land of opportunity due to famine or economic hardship in their homelands. By contrast, the Middle East in the late 19th and early 20th centuries had a relatively strong economy. To be sure, Arab Christians probably were not fond of the Muslim rule of the Ottoman Empire, but it was a period of relative prosperity for the region as a whole. The ruling Turks, however, forced heavy tax burdens on their people, which caused economic hardships even in good times.

Arab people of all religions had heard stories of the riches that could be found on American soil. One source for such stories was the 1876 Philadelphia Centennial Exposition. Among the exhibits from all over the world was the Turkish Pavilion, which featured numerous Arabs displaying their native arts and crafts. The American people gobbled up their wares, and the Syrians received their first taste of the riches that awaited them in America. Some returned home carrying goods from the West and stories of their prosperity, while others never left, choosing instead to travel the countryside peddling their wares.

For Arab Christians, the decision to leave for a largely Christian nation was much easier than it was for Muslims of the time. After all, they could be fairly certain that they wouldn't be persecuted for their religious beliefs upon their arrival. For Muslims, the decision was more difficult; they were uncertain about how their customs would be received in this new land. This group may have gotten its final push around 1908, when the Ottoman Empire began drafting Muslims into its army. Many Muslims are believed to have left for America to avoid serving in the military.

But there was also opportunity to be found in America—and a quick buck to be made. In fact, many of those who came to North America during this time did so with the feeling that their stay would only be temporary. Their plan was to arrive, make as much money as they could as quickly as they could, and return to their homeland to live the good life. They had heard of the riches that could be accumulated in America, and their heritage as a culture of peddlers

WHO ARE ARABS?

There are believed to be about three million Arab Americans in the United States today, but it's difficult to say how accurate that number is. Because of the ever-changing political landscape in Arab lands, changes in borders, and changes in classifications by the U.S. Census Bureau, the true number of Arabs in America has become blurred.

Today, the Census Bureau's definition indicates that Arab Americans come from portions of northern Africa (Algeria, Egypt, Libya, Morocco, Sudan, Tunisia) and western Asia (Bahrain, Iraq, Jordan, Kuwait, Lebanon, Oman, Palestine, Qatar, Saudi Arabia, Syria, United Arab Emirates, Yemen). These lands are often grouped today under the single term "Middle East."

The first wave of immigration from Arab lands came largely from the Syrian province of the Ottoman Empire. As a result, most of these people were referred to as "Syrians" rather than "Arabs." However, many were misclassified upon entering the U.S., which caused their numbers to be miscounted. In the early 1900s, those from Palestine were considered Palestinians. But in 1948, Palestinians lost official designation of their birthplace because of the creation of Israel in Palestine.

Because of the variety of different lands from which Arabs originate, their appearance varies greatly as well. While many are olive-skinned, some Arabs are white and some are black. About 90 percent of the immigrants from the first wave were Christians; immigrants today could be either Christian or Muslim.

made it seem attractive. Those who didn't favor peddling quickly found work in America's booming industrial centers; the modern factory was just coming into being.

This photograph, taken in the 1880s, shows horsemen of the Imperial Cavalry of the Ottoman Empire. The Ottoman Empire, based in Turkey, ruled the Arab lands from the 15th century until after World War I ended in 1918.

Instead of heading for home after establishing themselves and building a foundation, they sent word of their success to their relatives and encouraged them to follow. Before long, *emigration* went from single people leaving to entire families and villages packing up and traveling together. More than 100,000 Syrians found their way to North America by 1914.

Most of these Arabs were not professionals—they came from largely agricultural areas. But they planned to use their additional skills as craftspeople and peddlers to make their way in the New World. Another large group of immigrants left at the end of World War I, when the Allied forces divided up the fallen Ottoman Empire. In 1924, however, the Johnson-Reed Immigration Act set limits on the number of people who could come into America from other nations. The Syrian limit was set at exactly 100 people per year, which effectively ended the first wave of immigration. ✸

Arab Americans march in support of the United States after Friday prayers on September 21, 2001, in Brooklyn, New York. Most Arab Americans condemned the terrorist attacks on September 11 that destroyed the World Trade Center, damaged the Pentagon, and killed thousands of people. Although the attacks were the work of religious fanatics, some Arab Americans found themselves the target of attacks by their fellow citizens.

3 The Long Journey

At the beginning of this migration from Syrian lands to North America, the Arab people were able to leave their native lands and board ships for the United States largely **unfettered**. The Ottoman government didn't actively restrict Arabs from leaving their homeland. However, as the numbers of Syrians leaving began to grow, they began to find it harder to get there. Mass migration was taking a toll on the economy in the area, as fewer workers were available. That was costing the Ottoman government tax money—and power—so the ruling Turks posted soldiers to guard roads leading out of the region. The Syrians, however, weren't going to be stopped. They sneaked away at night, bribed guards, and swam or took small boats out to meet ships.

Money was another obstacle that needed to be overcome. While the region was relatively prosperous during this period, few people who left for the New World had large sums of money with which to do it. Families often scraped together as much money as they could just to send one family member overseas. They hoped their relative would find prosperity in America and return home to share it. Instead, these **emissaries** planted the seeds for generations of Arab Americans to come. As they found wealth—or at least success—as peddlers or factory workers, they sent money back home. With the money came

Muslim men pray at the Islamic Cultural Center in New York City before the start of their holy month, called Ramadan. During the month, observant Muslims abstain from eating, drinking, smoking, and other activities between sunrise and sunset.

stories of the riches and opportunity that existed in the New World, and the families soon followed.

However, these Arab pioneers also had to endure hardships during their journey. Just like their counterparts from other countries who sought out the same opportunity in the U.S., their travels were often a test of strength and will. They traveled in the lowest level of accommodations aboard ship, called steerage. In an effort to capitalize on the desire of these immigrants to reach America, ship operators would pack as many people as possible into the ships. Quite often, they were packed in like animals, without adequate food, water, or sanitation. The result was a long journey that was unsanitary at best and dangerously unhealthy at worst. Many immigrants never made it to the new land, dying along the way.

Others encountered suffering of another kind at the hands of greedy ship operators: they were simply sent to a different country. Many Syrians were convinced they were boarding ships for America that were, in fact, headed elsewhere—some not even to the North American continent. There were many Syrian immigrants who sailed across the ocean dreaming of New York, only to arrive in South America. When that happened, some would board another ship for the correct destination, while others would simply make the best of it and settle where they were. One such group had been rerouted to Canada in the late 1800s and ended up settling in Montreal after finding success as peddlers. Their accident resulted in the founding of a small Arab community there.

However, the majority did land in the U.S., most of them in New York. As the years went on, new arrivals through Ellis Island would find a strong base of fellow Arabs in New York City. Here they would recover from their journey, make the connections they needed to find work or the supplies necessary for peddling, and begin to spread out across the land. ✳

A patriotic T-shirt hangs in a van parked in front of a strip mall in Dearborn, Michigan. Dearborn, a suburb of Detroit, is home to one of the largest Arabic communities outside of the Middle East.

Life as a Peddler

As the first wave of Syrian immigrants was arriving in America, they were joined by many other groups of newcomers. Thousands of immigrants were arriving at Ellis Island and other ports on the east coast. They settled into neighborhoods in New York City or the surrounding area and, in many cases, recreated their previous homeland in the American environment. Neighborhoods quickly took on the ethnic culture of their residents—an Irish neighborhood here, a Little Italy there. Most of these other ethnic groups were able to blend in to the New York City environment without being noticed as newcomers—that is, until they spoke.

The Arabs who were arriving on American shores had many similarities to these other groups, but there were some profound differences as well. Syrian neighborhoods did spring up in New York and near other ports, but they were generally more *transient* and not as firmly rooted. Their clothing also set them apart, as many of them arrived in traditional robes. Further, their skin color—generally olive skin—differentiated them from the vast majority of people they saw when they arrived. Their culture, customs, and, in some cases, religion also was different from the people they first encountered.

Perhaps the biggest thing that differentiated these Syrian immigrants from the Europeans of the same era was the type of work

SPREADING OUT ACROSS THE LAND

Arab Americans live in every state in the U.S. and some parts of Canada. Because they have tended toward entrepreneurial and industrial occupations, the majority of Arab people can be found in or near the major cities that serve as the corporate centers in America. For the most part farming and other more rural occupations have not drawn Arab people.

More than two-thirds of Arab Americans live in just 10 states: California, Illinois, Maryland, Michigan, New Jersey, New York, Ohio, Texas, Virginia, and Massachusetts. Three metropolitan areas in the U.S.—Los Angeles, New York, and Detroit—account for about one-third of all Arab Americans.

New York City has been the greatest point of entry to North America for people from Arab lands, dating all the way back to the beginning of the first wave of immigration in the late 1800s. New York and neighboring New Jersey remain the main point of entry, and New York has been considered the center of the cultural and commercial aspects of Arab life in this part of the world. It is not, however, home to the largest population of Arab Americans. Southern California has earned the distinction of being the primary destination, or settling point, for Arab people.

they chose to undertake. While their European counterparts headed for industrial jobs in large numbers—helping America's booming industrial revolution in the process—Syrians kept a more traditional approach to earning a living. To be sure, some did go to work in factories around the U.S., but a large number became "pack peddlers."

This drawing from the early 19th century provides the western image of an Arab merchant, who is wearing a turban and a blue-and-white striped outer garment over a long belted tunic. Many Arabs who came to the United States in the 19th century worked as peddlers, selling goods throughout the country.

A pack peddler is someone who carries a large pack on his back and walks from neighborhood to neighborhood, town to town, city to city, selling goods out of the pack. Syrians were a largely independent group, and their desire to be on their own fueled their success as peddlers. It could be grueling and sometimes dangerous work, but peddling became a way of life—and a way to wealth—for a large number of these early Syrian immigrants.

At this time, getting products from the manufacturers to people in far-flung locations was not nearly as easy as it is today. A person couldn't simply pick up the phone and place an order—even the catalog industry was just getting developed. New methods of transportation were developing, but none were so developed as to make distribution of products as simple as it is today.

So the peddler served a purpose for industry. Some peddlers would get their supplies from huge warehouses or manufacturers, while others would simply sell items they had made themselves or those that were made by relatives in their village. Often, new Syrians arriving in New York would quickly hook up with a Syrian supplier, rest up briefly to regain their strength from the long voyage, then head out peddling. As they ran out of supplies on their journey, they would arrive at a small

An Arab stonemason works carefully to restore ornate stonework. Arab immigrants to North America worked in many jobs after they arrived in the United States and Canada.

peddling settlement in a new city to refill their inventory. They sold a wide variety of items, from toiletries to sewing supplies to trinkets to handmade jewelry. Some sold cloth or clothing.

The danger of their job came from the fact that they weren't always well received. Many peddlers were chased away from homes or farms— their strange language and appearance viewed as a threat by the homeowner. But people in rural communities, where life was more tedious, often counted the days between appearances by these pack peddlers. Their arrival would be treated like that of visiting royalty; welcomed quickly into the home, they were often offered a place to sleep for the night and a hot meal.

Peddling required a certain personality, one that was able to make homesteaders comfortable and not feel threatened, yet with enough salesmanship to be able to get the job done. Many of these peddlers became excellent storytellers. The peddlers' needs were simple: to make a sale, find a place to spend the night, and, if they were lucky, get some food. Women peddlers were often the most successful; they were not considered to be as threatening and the American customs of the time made it more likely they would be offered a place to stay.

As they traveled across the United States and went into the homes of thousands of Americans, they were able to learn more about the culture and, perhaps more importantly, the language of their new home. New York was not their only starting point, either. If they landed at another port, they simply worked from there, spreading out across whatever land they happened to encounter. ✳

5 Settlements and Settling Down

When Arab Americans arrived at another settlement, they would often stay put for a few days. These settlements, often run by the suppliers who kept the peddlers stocked, became thriving camps of transient peddlers. They would stop and share their best stories from their journey and the adventures they had had in this town or that. Filled as they were with fellow Arab people, these settlements would give the peddlers a little piece of home. These settlements were often the beginning of what would become thriving Syrian neighborhoods, many of which still exist today.

They generally were located in towns with bustling economies fueled by other industry—but not near major cities. It was too easy for residents of major cities to get the goods they needed, so the peddlers needed a rural or small-town environment to find success. When they had made a good deal of money, many would stop in new areas and set up their own peddling settlement by graduating from peddler to supplier. Others who found success did what many successful businesses do—they expanded. Some would buy horses and carts to pull along

Muslim men leave the Islamic Center in Washington, D.C. The structure, which was built in 1949, features a minaret that is 160 feet tall.

their expanded supply line. These peddlers could travel further and more quickly, giving them the ability to reach customers others might never find.

They also added new, more expensive products to their inventory, including larger items, such as imported rugs, that would have been impossible to carry in a pack. And their industry was booming, especially in the period leading up to World War I. Even an average peddler would make as much as 50 percent more than the average factory worker. In many cases, the profits were used to bring family members over from the homeland.

As time passed, the very companies whose products the peddlers were spreading across the countryside gobbled up the peddling industry. As mail order became a staple and catalogs began regularly arriving in American homes, people no longer needed a peddler to show up on their doorstep. Even in small cities, department stores replaced the peddlers, as people were able to get many different types of items in a single stop.

Syrian independence didn't suffer, however. In fact, many peddlers simply put down their packs and became merchants—opening grocery stores, bakeries, clothing stores, and other businesses. Others finally gave in and turned to factory work, taking a steady paycheck and a regular schedule over the harsh life of wandering the countryside carrying a pack. When they did, the experience they had gained with the American culture through their travels allowed them to quickly become a part of the communities in which they chose to live.

A young Arab boy studies the Koran, the holy book of Islam. Although for the most part Arab Americans have become assimilated into American culture, they have retained many aspects of their religious and cultural heritage.

What were once peddling settlements grew to become vibrant Arab-American communities. Churches began to spring up to support the active needs of Christian Arabs. Organizations to support Arabs in America also sprouted, as did newspapers printed in both English and Arabic. Shopkeeping was the primary source of income for these Arab immigrants—most of them owning dry goods stores that sold goods similar to those they carried when they were peddlers.

In the United States, mosques are often built to match the surrounding architecture. The Dar Al-Islam mosque in Abiquiu, New Mexico, is a good example. While it incorporates a dome, as traditional mosques do, the Dar Al-Islam mosque includes distinctly southwestern elements in its design as well.

The entire family pitched in to help with the operation; in many cases, the family lived in an apartment above the store. The children helped stock the shelves and sweep the floors as soon as they were old enough to do so. Generally, the men ran the stores while the women ran the households and, in some cases, even made some of the goods that were sold. They clung to the family and to their traditions, and most of the businesses they ran bore the family name.

As time passed, however, the second generation of these immigrants began to become more a part of American life. Children sought American education, married people of other ethnic backgrounds, and set out on their own to find their own way in the world instead of raising their family in their parents' home. This was particularly true among Christian Arabs, who were able to find mates with the same religious beliefs despite different ethnic backgrounds. The more liberal American lifestyle, especially during the "Roaring Twenties," pulled this second generation away from its roots. Attending American schools also showed them a different way of looking at things. During World War I, the Arabs who served in the American military also had a heightened sense of belonging to their new country. ✳

A veiled Arab woman holds her son. The second wave of Arab immigration to the United States included more Muslims than Christians. Many Arabs have come to North America in the past 30 years.

6 The Second Wave

The second wave of immigrants from Arab lands to North America began after World War II. This group has many similarities to the first wave of immigrants, but there are some sharp contrasts as well. While the first group was 90 percent Christian, this second wave featured a majority of Muslims. The first group was largely uneducated and somewhat transient; the second group was well educated and came seeking more education. But like their predecessors, this second wave of Arab immigrants fled political and economic strife and came to North America seeking new opportunity. Ironically, many of them planned to come only for a short time but ended up staying for a lifetime, just like those who came before them.

The Middle East has been the source of political turmoil for generations, much of it affecting the rest of the world. This second wave of immigrants were often members of their nations' upper classes—important city-dwelling families who were fleeing countries in which leadership had changed, sometimes violently. Many were Palestinians who lost their homeland when Israel was established as a country in 1948. Many of these immigrants were already English-speaking people, having attended Western schools.

However, more than 75 percent of this second wave of immigration came after 1967, when Israel defeated Syria, Egypt, and Jordan in the

ARAB PEOPLE AT THE FORD MOTOR COMPANY

The first wave of Arab immigrants to the U.S. and Canada gravitated toward peddling as a means to make money. Many of them were very successful at it. But another large group of Arab Americans headed toward jobs in industry.

Muslims, in particular, were drawn to this type of work. Industrial centers began to draw them in large numbers, and many of these areas continue to have large Arab populations today. One perfect example is Dearborn, Michigan, which boasts one of the largest settlements of Arab people in the U.S. Dearborn is home to the Ford Motor Company, which, in 1914, began to pay factory workers as much as $5 per day for eight hours of work. This was a good sum in those days, and it drew the Muslim-Arab population there in large numbers in the ensuing years.

Dearborn, which is a suburb of Detroit, today has one of the largest and most condensed populations of Arab Americans in North America. Many neighborhoods there are primarily Arabic; in fact, Arab Americans make up more than 20 percent of the city's population and more than 40 percent of the school-aged children.

A former CEO and president of Ford Motor Company was Jacques Nasser, who is an Arab American.

Six-Day War. The Immigration Act of 1965, which ended the quota system that had previously limited the number of people who could come to America from Arab lands, laid the groundwork for this huge flow of immigrants.

Since 1967, this constant flow has allowed thousands of Arab people to escape the fighting that has plagued their homelands. They came to America to benefit from its educational system or to enter into the business world. Having a much stronger foundation in American life than earlier immigrants did, this second group adjusted much more quickly. Coming as they did from generally wealthier families, they

A group of soldiers pauses on the Golan Heights, Syria, during the Six-Day War in 1967. By the time fighting ended on June 10, 1967, Israel had won a large area of territory from its Arab neighbors. Constant warfare in the Middle East has inspired many Arabs to leave their homelands and make a new start in the United States or Canada.

ARABS AND RELIGION

Many people falsely believe that all Arabs are Muslims. This couldn't be further from the truth. In fact, the vast majority of the first wave of immigration from Arab lands were Syrian Christians. About 90 percent of those who immigrated to North America from the late 1800s to the beginning of World War I are believed to have been Christian.

Muslims are those who practice the religion known as Islam. They are followers of the prophet Muhammad, who was born around A.D. 570 in the city of Mecca. Islam includes some of the beliefs of its predecessors, Judaism and Christianity. However, Muslims have a number of religious traditions that compete with

America's societal values. For example, Islamic beliefs center on modesty and prohibit marriage between people of different faiths. Still, Muslims are the fastest-growing segment of the Arab-American community. The second wave of immigration from the Middle East included a larger number of Muslims. However, about two-thirds of the current Arab-American population is Christian.

were able to enter the American educational system and pay for college or post-graduate education more readily than those who came before them. These people headed for largely urban areas, where they found work easily. This helped fuel the development of the thriving Arab community in the Los Angeles, California area—the largest concentration of Arab people in North America.

Those who weren't as skilled headed for industrial centers to find the Arab communities that remained in existence from the earlier wave of immigration. These blue-collar workers provided a new base of Arab people to places like Dearborn, Michigan, which had previously benefited from Ford Motor Company's need for factory workers. Dearborn today contains the second-largest population of Arabs in the United States. This second wave of immigration also sparked a revival of traditional Arab customs and spawned a greater presence for the Muslim church in America. At the same time, these Arab people had greater respect for the governments they left behind and a greater awareness of the troubles of their homeland.

The Middle East required more attention from Americans during the 1970s and 1980s as well. American reliance on oil from the region and a variety of conflicts between the U.S. government and various governments there caused Americans to view the Arab nations in a more negative light. As a result, Arab people faced a heightened level of discrimination years after their counterparts from other ethnic backgrounds had put such worries behind them. Negative portrayals in the media and elsewhere of Arab people as

ARAB AMERICAN PROFILE: RALPH NADER

A two-word phrase is nearly always used alongside Ralph Nader's name: consumer advocate. While Nader did not invent the idea, he helped to revolutionize it and to empower consumers as they had never been before.

Nader was born February 27, 1934, the son of Lebanese immigrants who operated a restaurant and bakery. Nader began to stand out during his undergraduate years at Princeton, when he attempted to rally student support on a number of issues. He graduated in 1955 and attended Harvard Law School, where he developed a dislike for irresponsible corporations and the attorneys who represented them.

At Harvard, Nader first examined the safety of automobiles, writing an article in *The Nation* called, "The Safe Car You Can't Buy." He wrote, "It is clear Detroit today is designing automobiles for style, cost, performance and calculated obsolescence, but not…for safety." In 1965, he published his famous book, *Unsafe at Any Speed: The Designed-in Dangers of the American Automobile*. The book didn't hit the big time until an article in *The New Republic* outlined General Motors' underhanded attempts to discredit Nader. He was catapulted into the public spotlight and became a celebrity, and he used his newfound clout to push Americans to become more involved in the consumer issues that affect their very lives.

Nader built student task forces to crusade against bureaucracy and consumer fraud. The first such group produced a report on the Federal Trade Commission that resulted in a major overhaul of the bureaucracy. Later groups came to be known as "Nader's Raiders." Throughout his career, Nader made an attempt to protect American citizens from waste, greed, and indifference in both government and private corporations. In 2000, as the candidate of the Green Party, he made an unsuccessful run for president of the United States.

terrorists made life much more difficult for many Arab people, especially those who clung to traditional modes of dress and other customs. Here, the second wave's increased educational background played a key role. They united to form new Arab-American organizations that have helped to protect Arab interests in America and bring together Arabs of different generations. Organizations such as the Association of Arab American University Graduates, the National Association of Arab Americans, and the Arab American Institute helped unite Arab people and present a more positive view of Arab people to the American public.

As all this was going on, this second wave took its place alongside the first group as shopkeepers, business owners, entrepreneurs, and more. And, like their *predecessors*, their children quickly adapted to American life and became Americanized.

Arab Americans in the United States faced a new challenge after September 11, 2001. On that date, two groups of terrorists flew hijacked airplanes into the twin towers of the World Trade Center in New York City. The towers were destroyed and thousands of people working in them were killed. A third terrorist team crashed a hijacked plane into the Pentagon, the Washington, D.C., offices of the United States' armed forces. A fourth airplane was also taken over by terrorists; it crashed in the Pennsylvania countryside, killing all aboard. All of the terrorists were from Arab countries; a Saudi Arabian terrorist named Osama bin Laden had financed their training and their deadly mission.

Americans were shocked and angered at the surprise attack and its tragic results. Arab Americans joined with their countrymen in condemning the attacks. However, some ignorant people attacked Arab Americans, as well as other people who looked as though they were from the Middle East or Central Asia, such as Pakistanis and Indians. There were a few cases where rocks were thrown through the windows of mosques in the United States, or offensive graffiti was sprayed on exterior walls. Thankfully, the violence against Arab

ARAB AMERICAN DEMOGRAPHICS

One can find Arab Americans in all walks of life, in all parts of the country, with all kinds of different backgrounds. Like Asian Americans, Arab Americans come from a number of different countries, and thus they were influenced by a wide range of customs, trends, beliefs, and so on. In America today, demographic information paints a picture of the Arab American as well educated, professional, and relatively well-off financially.

Compared to the American population at large (that is, the average American), Arab Americans are better educated. The second wave of immigrants, who arrived within the last 40 years, generally had achieved a high level of education before coming to the West. Some came for the express purpose of pursuing higher education.

Household income averages are generally higher for Arab Americans than for the population as a whole. However, one in five Arab immigrants has a household income of less than the poverty level. In general, however, those Arab Americans who are either U.S. born or U.S. citizens have a higher income level than first-generation immigrants who have not become citizens.

Three Arab-American women leave a memorial service for the victims of the September 11, 2001, terrorist attack on the World Trade Center and Pentagon. Although Arab Americans condemned the attacks, some became victims of violence by fellow citizens.

Americans was not widespread. Nevertheless, in the wake of September 11 many Arab-American citizens were nervous that they might become the target of attacks.

As strife continues in the Middle East, Arab immigration to the United States continues as well. According to the 2000 U.S. Census, there are more than 3 million Americans of Arab descent. Statistics also indicate there are more than 200,000 people of Arab descent living in Canada as of that country's 2001 census. The ever-growing Arab-American community continues to thrive in the New World.

Chronology

1717 Arabic-speaking slaves begin to arrive in the United States.

1787 Morocco becomes the first country to recognize the independence of the United States; Mahammed III signs a "Treaty of Friendship and Cooperation" with Washington.

1840 The first cargo load of goods from the lands known as Oman and Muscat arrive in New York Harbor on the ship *Sultanah*.

1856 A ship arrives in Indianola, Texas, carrying 33 camels that had been purchased by the United States government for use by the army. After a seven-year trial, the government determined that camels were not fit for army transportation during war.

1876 The Centennial Exposition held in Philadelphia attracts Arab merchants, who are so successful selling goods to Americans that their success helps spawn the first wave of Arab immigration to North America.

1885 The first wave of Arab immigration, made up largely of Arab Christians begins.

1892 The first Arabic language newspaper in America, *Kawkab Amerika,* begins publication.

1893 The Columbian Exposition in Chicago draws another wave of merchants to display their wares; these merchants are also successful, and many stay on to establish peddling settlements in the Great Lakes region.

1900 The Syrian population in Manhattan and Brooklyn surpasses 10,000.

1904 The St. Louis Exposition brings another group of merchants from Arab lands. The ice cream cone makes its debut, thanks to a Syrian waffle maker who aids an ice cream vendor who had run out of plates.

1907 An Immigration Department report indicates that Syrians send home more money per capita than the immigrants from any other country, and that 94 percent of Syrian immigrants who came to America were joining relatives already here; the first Syrian-American club is established.

1914 Immigration from Arab lands begins to drop substantially.

1924 The Johnson-Reed Immigration Act sets limits on the number of people who can come to America from various countries. It favors European countries and limits the number of Syrians to 100 per year.

1936 The Arab League in America is founded.

1945 The Arab-American Institute is founded; the second wave of immigration begins.

1948 Israel is established as a country, and many Palestinians flee their homeland for America.

1949 The Islamic Center is completed in Washington, D.C.

1952 The Federation of Islamic Associations in the United States and Canada is created.

1965 The Immigration Act of 1965 is passed, ending the limits that were previously in place on numbers of immigrants from specific countries.

1967 Israel defeats Syria, Egypt, and Jordan in the Six-Day War, launching a huge influx of new Arab immigrants.

1973 The National Association of Arab Americans is founded.

2001 On September 11, terrorists destroy the World Trade Center in New York City and damage the Pentagon in Washington, D.C. Thousands of people are killed. Arab Americans condemn the attacks, which were carried out by Arab Muslim extremists. There are a few cases in which Arab Americans are attacked by their fellow citizens, although these are not widespread.

2003 The Arab-American population of the United States is estimated at more than 3 million; Canada is believed to be home for more than 200,000 Arab Canadians.

Famous Arab Americans

POLITICS

Ralph Nader consumer advocate and former presidential candidate

Pat Danner Missouri congresswoman

John Sununu former White House Chief of Staff

Donna Shalala former Secretary of Health and Human Services

George Mitchell former Senate Majority Leader

SPORTS

Doug Flutie former Heisman Trophy winner and NFL quarterback

Jeff George NFL quarterback

Bobby Rahal 1986 Indy 500 champion

Jim Harrick college basketball coach who won national title with UCLA in 1995

Joe Robbie former owner of the Miami Dolphins

ENTERTAINMENT

Paul Anka singer/entertainer

Paula Abdul dancer/singer

Frank Zappa singer

Jamie Farr actor

Danny Thomas actor/entertainer

Marlo Thomas actress

Salma Hayek actress

Kathy Najimy actress

F. Murray Abraham Academy Award-winning actor

William Peter Blatty author, *The Exorcist*

BUSINESS

J.M. Haggar founder of the Haggar clothing company

Jacques Nasser president and CEO of Ford Motor Company

Joseph Abboud menswear designer

Paul Orfalea founder of Kinko's copy stores

Ray Jallow economist

OTHERS

Candy Lightner founder of Mothers Against Drunk Driving

Dr. Hussam A. Fadhli award-winning sculptor

Steven Naifeh winner of the Pulitzer Prize for biography for *Jackson Pollock: An American Saga*

Dr. Ahmed H. Zewail winner of the Nobel Prize for chemistry in 1999

Dr. Elias Corey winner of the Nobel Prize for chemistry in 1990

Dr. Farouk el-Baz helped plan the Apollo moon landings

Christa McAulife teacher who died in the explosion of the Space Shuttle *Challenger*

Glossary

Affiliate to be in association or close relationship with.

Capitalize to take advantage of something.

Discrimination to treat someone poorly for some reason other than on merit.

Dupe to persuade or convince someone to do something by trickery or deception.

Emigration to leave one's homeland to settle in another country.

Emissary an agent or representative sent on a particular mission.

Ethnic a group of people with similar homelands and customs.

Immigrant a person who comes to a new country after leaving his or her homeland.

Muslim a follower of the religion of Islam; occasionally spelled Moslem.

Peddle to travel from place to place, selling goods out of a pack or a cart.

Persecution to cause another person to suffer in some way because of their beliefs.

Predecessor something previously in use or existence that has been replaced or succeeded by something else.

Steerage the lowest-level accommodations on a ship.

Strife bitter and sometimes violent conflict or struggle.

Terrorist a person who uses threats or violence as a means to achieve a goal.

Transient a person or people who move from place to place regularly without staying long in any one area.

Turks the people in the ruling class during the Ottoman Empire were known as Turks, because the land at that time was part of Turkey.

Unfettered not subject to limits or restrictions.

Wares things offered for sale.

Further Reading

Abraham, Sameer Y., and Nabeel Abraham, editors. *Arabs in the New World: Studies on Arab-American Communities*. Detroit: Wayne State University, 1983.

Bentz, Thomas. *New Immigrants*. New York: Pilgrim Press, 1981.

Kadi, Joanna. *Food for Our Grandmothers*. Writings by Arab-Americans and Arab-Canadians. Boston: South End Press, 1994.

Naff, Alixa. *The Arab Americans*. Philadelphia: Chelsea House Publishers, 1999.

Patai, Raphael. *The Arab Mind*. New York: Macmillan Publishing Company, 1973.

Portes, Alejandro, and Rumbaut, Ruben. *Immigrant America*. Berkeley and Los Angeles: University of California Press, 1990.

Salins, Peter D. *Assimilation American Style*. New York: Basic Books, 1997.

Turner Mehdi, Beverlee. *The Arabs in America 1492–1977*. Dobbs Ferry: Oceana Publications, Inc. 1978.

Tracing Your Arab-American Ancestors

Carmack, Sharon DeBartolo. *A Genealogist's Guide to Discovering Your Immigrant and Ethnic Ancestors*. Cincinnati: Betterway Books, 2000.

Greenwood, Val D. *The Researcher's Guide to American Genealogy*. 3rd ed. Baltimore: Genealogical Publishing Co., 2000.

Mindel, Charles, Robert W. Habenstein, and Roosevelt Wright Jr., editors. *Ethnic Families in America: Patterns and Variations*. New York: Prentice-Hall, 1997.

Internet Resources

http://www.census.gov

The official website of the U.S. Bureau of the Census contains information about the most recent census taken in 2000.

http://www.statcan.ca/start.html

The website for Canada's Bureau of Statistics, which includes population information updated for the most recent census in July 2001.

http://www.aaiusa.org/

This is the Web site for the American Arab Institute and features leadership training and strategies in electoral politics and policy issues that concern Arab Americans.

http://www.ralphnader.com

This Web site contains everything you need to know about Ralph Nader, including his career highlights, opinions and editorials he has written, and press releases.

Index

Photo Credits

Contributors

Barry Moreno has been librarian and historian at the Ellis Island Immigration Museum and the Statue of Liberty National Monument since 1988. He is the author of *The Statue of Liberty Encyclopedia*, which was published by Simon & Schuster in October 2000. He is a native of Los Angeles, California. After graduation from California State University at Los Angeles, where he earned a degree in history, he joined the National Park Service as a seasonal park ranger at the Statue of Liberty; he eventually became the monument's librarian. In his spare time, Barry enjoys reading, writing, and studying foreign languages and grammar. His biography has been included in *Who's Who Among Hispanic Americans*, *The Directory of National Park Service Historians*, *Who's Who in America*, and *The Directory of American Scholars*.

Bob Temple is the president of Red Line Editorial, Inc., an editorial services company based in the Minneapolis-St. Paul area. He is the author of 22 books ranging from children's non-fiction to computer how-to titles.